# Going to the Market

by Jeanne Tao

Illustrated by Jaime Zollars

Glenview, Illinois • Boston, Massachusetts • Chandler, Arizona
Upper Saddle River, New Jersey

Mama made a list of food. She asked Lisa and Jenny to buy it. The food was for dinner. "Be careful," said Mama.

"We will buy curry first," said Lisa.
"What is curry?" asked Jenny.
"Curry is a spice. It gives flavor to food," said Lisa.

The girls went to the store. "We need some curry, please," said Lisa to Mr. Sharma.

He gave them a box. Lisa paid Mr. Sharma. Jenny carried the bag.

"We will buy tomatoes next," said Lisa. "Mrs. Rios sells vegetables at the market."
"I like tomatoes!" said Jenny.

The girls went to the market. "We need tomatoes, please," said Lisa to Mrs. Rios.

Mrs. Rios gave them the tomatoes. Lisa paid her. Jenny carried the bag.

"We will buy fish next," said Lisa. "Mr. Li sells fish here."

"I like fish!" said Jenny.

The girls went to see Mr. Li. "We need some fish, please," said Lisa to Mr. Li.

Mr. Li gave them a fish. Lisa paid him. Jenny carried the bag.

"We need parsley next," said Lisa.
"Do you know what it is?"

"It is a small, green plant," said Jenny.
"I didn't see any at the market."

The girls walked home. They saw Mrs. Jones.

"We bought food for Mama. But we didn't find parsley," said Jenny.

"I grow parsley in my garden," said Mrs. Jones.

Mrs. Jones gave the girls some parsley.
"Thank you!" said Lisa.
The girls said good-bye. Jenny carried the bag.

"Did you get everything?" Mama asked.
"Yes," said Lisa.
"And I carried ALL of the bags!" said Jenny.